THIS IS ME!

2022

VOICES UNHEARD

Edited By Allie Jones

First published in Great Britain in 2022 by:

 Young**Writers**® Est. 1991

Young Writers
Remus House
Coltsfoot Drive
Peterborough
PE2 9BF
Telephone: 01733 890066
Website: www.youngwriters.co.uk

Printed and bound in the UK by BookPrintingUK
Website: www.bookprintinguk.com
YB0517J

FOREWORD

*For Young Writers' latest competition This Is Me,
we asked primary school pupils to look inside
themselves, to think about what makes them unique,
and then write a poem about it! They rose to the
challenge magnificently and the result is this fantastic
collection of poems in a variety of poetic styles.*

Here at Young Writers our aim is to encourage creativity
in children and to inspire a love of the written word, so
it's great to get such an amazing response, with some
absolutely fantastic poems. It's important for children to
focus on and celebrate themselves and this competition
allowed them to write freely and honestly, celebrating
what makes them great, expressing their hopes and
fears, or simply writing about their favourite things.
This Is Me gave them the power of words. The result
is a collection of inspirational and moving poems that
also showcase their creativity and writing ability.

*I'd like to congratulate all the young poets
in this anthology, I hope this inspires them
to continue with their creative writing.*

CONTENTS

Thea Beales (7)	65
Theo Neophytou (8)	66
Ashton Forchione (8)	67
Gabriella Ehujor (8)	68
Alexis-Mae Peck (8)	69
Harper Morris (8)	70
Iris Correia (8)	71
Josiah Joseph (8)	72
Junior Makombe (8)	73
Tyler Burkhill (8)	74
Isabel Booth (7)	75
Terry Breese-Ellis (8)	76
Olivia Sheen (8)	77
Muhammad Usayd Ali (8)	78
Caroline Norman (7)	79
Dayyan Shakeel (8)	80
Finley Newbery (8)	81
Georgina Owusu Tabiri (7)	82
Al-Rayaan Khan (8)	83
Andrew van der Merwe (8)	84
Heath McCracken (8)	85
Maria Bibi (7)	86
Finley Seymour (8)	87
Manha Moazzam (8)	88
Carter Leone (8)	89
Charlie Ladbrooke (8)	90
Theo Jeeves (8)	91
Aamari Esimaje (7)	92
Maira Basharat (8)	93
Bilal Khazeem (8)	94
Mariaa Khalil (8)	95
Gavin Carcedo (8)	96
Alfie Walker (8)	97
Joey Thirkettle (8)	98

Carnalridge Primary School, Portrush

Kaiya Andrew-Mowat (10)	99
Maya Kelly (10)	100
Hannah McCormick (9)	102
Alexander Taylor (10)	104
Alastair Campbell (10)	106
Julia Fornara (10)	108

Catherine Rainey (10)	109
Sarah McCaughey (10)	110
Daisy Ridley Anderson (10)	111
Rio McDonald (10)	112
Amelia McCaughern (10)	113

Hampton Hargate Primary School, Hampton Hargate

Eshaal Fatima Merchant (9)	114
Alexa Abbott-New (8)	117
Felicity Joe (9)	118
Annalise Edwards (8)	120
Kaobim Anajekwu (8)	121
Maddison Beeke (9)	122
Eve Taylor (9)	123
Muhammad Rayyan Siddiqi (9)	124
Hailie Chilman (9)	125
William Liddle (9)	126
Tymoteusz Sietnik (9)	127
Haasika Vishnuprabhu (9)	128
Maisie Walthew (8)	129
Nishta Bhatia (9)	130
Lois Cook (9)	131
Lara Wilkins (9)	132
Niamh Jones (9)	133
Gabriel Nimakoh (9)	134
Sauvik Srivastava (9)	135
David Marian Belu (9)	136
Joshua Lorde (8)	137
Tulula Rushmer (9)	138
Ria Azar (9)	139
Albert Gabroveanu (9)	140
Amber Louise Lemmon (9)	141
Joanna Akintola (9)	142
Harriet Lawrence (8)	143
Lucas Peters (9)	144
Liam King (9)	145
Emīlija Millere (8)	146
Leonardo Kakosch (9)	147
Kayde Di Gorno (8)	148
Maeva Mitchell (9)	149
Renee Jarvis (9)	150
Megan Colbert (9)	151

Riyah Valani (9)	152
Lydia Pattison (8)	153
Hassan Shiraz (9)	154
Anna Donovan (9)	155
Zainab Naqvi (8)	156
Aysha Choudhry (9)	157
Louie Hawksford (9)	158
Alyssa Barrett (9)	159
Keerthigaa Senthilkumar (9)	160
Jack TD (9)	161
Jacob Sloan (9)	162
Daisy Hollingsworth (9)	163
Ella Raven (9)	164
Harry Flavill (9)	165
Sofia Rodulfo (9)	166
Noah Ferguson (8)	167
Farrell Martinez (9)	168
Riley Flaherty (8)	169

Holy Child Primary School, Creggan Estate

Shannon O'Hagan (10)	170
Killian Doherty (9)	171
Mia Chambers (10)	172
Fionn Friel (10)	173
Bobby (10)	174
Aubree Friel (10)	175
Alfie Gallagher	176
Jack Gallagher (10)	177
Caolan Moore	178

St Patrick's Primary School, Hilltown

Darcy Malcomson (10)	179
Grace Gribben (10)	180
Oisin McConville (10)	181
Patrick Morgan (10)	182
Jake Morgan (10)	183
Oisin McSherry (10)	184
Austin Matthews (10)	185
Daniel Duggan (9)	186
Tyler Dinsmore (9)	187

Luke Fearon (10)	188
Ryan Burns (10)	189
Jack Binks (9)	190
Kelsey Quinn (10)	191
Senan Quinn (10)	192
Ryan Devlin (10)	193

Sunny Bank Primary School, Sittingbourne

Alan Cychowski (10)	194
Chloe Eustace (10)	195
Lizziemarie Wilson (10)	196
Lilly Doyle (9)	197
Amelia Bolger (9)	198
Oliver Glenn (10)	199
Darcy Price (9)	200
George Butler (10)	201
Payton Grimwood (10)	202
Declan Bruce (9)	203
Taylor Friday (10)	204
Riley (10)	205
Jemma Tyler-Clarke (10)	206

THE POEMS

Autistic Me!

T itanic is my special interest

O bsessed with all things army

B rothers, I have one

I also have a sister

E xcitement fills me when I get American sweets, sometimes as a treat!

M an United are my team, one day I'll see them, that's my dream

A utistic is what they say I am, apparently I have a super brain

X -rays, I've had one!

W orld War II is my favourite topic

E ggs are my breakfast of choice, the yolk is yellow, my favourite colour

L emon is my thing, I love its zesty zing!

L auris, he's my best friend, the end!

Tobie Maxwell (7)
Abbey Primary School, Newtownards

This Is Me, Rosie!

My name is Rosie, I am eight years old
My birthday is 5th May
Can I tell you something you won't believe?
I climbed the biggest mountain can't you see?
My favourite one was Lamagan
It was steep and we cooked sausages on it.

I love to go paddle boarding and scuba diving off
the back you see
Going back to the tent, warming up by the fire and
toasting marshmallows
Then going mountain biking down trails with my
pink and purple full-face helmet.

Baking cookies is so much fun
Smartie ones, yum, yum, yum
I love to roll on my gymnastics bar I got for my
eighth birthday
It is super fun!
I love drawing, painting, sketching and making
photo frames
I'm very good at it and get supplies for my
birthday.

My favourite animal is a bunny,
When it comes to carrots, munch, munch, munch
I love to read books
Interesting ones get most of my looks
Me and Daddy are always first in the sea
Jumping about, body boarding you'll see.

So far to date I've lost eight teeth
I have something else to tell you - I love doing maths
I love to play with dolls
My favourite food is prawns and my favourite drink is Diet Coke
I love to do yoga!

Rosie McConville (8)
Abbey Primary School, Newtownards

My Perfect Day

I don't need an alarm, I'm the first one up.
Mum's still sleeping, but not my pup!
Come on Nina, up on the couch,
It's time to watch Operation Ouch!

Dad's up, Mum's still snoring.
The coffee machine's on, she'll soon get going.
My tummy is rumbling, pancakes, please?
I gobble them down with plenty of ease.

I'm ready to go, let's go for a walk.
I want to climb Slieve Donard,
But Mum just wants to talk!
Me and Dad make it, it's a long way up,
And somehow Dad managed to lose his sock!

We made it!
Picnic time.
Now we have to make our way down.
I've got a sledge, will that do?
Dad says he needs the loo!

Home at last, pizza time.
Let's put on a movie Dad said.
Now I'm ready for one more climb...
All the way up to bed!

Alasdair Hamilton (8)

Abbey Primary School, Newtownards

All About Nutty Noah

My name is Noah Bradley and I live in Portavogie with my family.
I go to Abbey Primary School and my maths skills they do rule.
My teachers Mrs Fulton and Mrs Brown are the best in the whole town.
I am very fast at running and my humour is just stunning.
In my bright orange kit for Ards Rangers I play football
And in-between the goalposts I stand tall.
Maybe one day when I'm older I will be sighted
In a red kit playing for United.
I love the Belfast Giants, they are the best team around
And I got to stand and cheer as champions they were crowned.

Noah Bradley (8)
Abbey Primary School, Newtownards

If I Were A Poem!

J umping Joshua loves to jump up and down on his trampoline.

O n a normal day you will see him in his Ju-Jitsu gee, hip throwing his friends and smiling with glee.

S ometimes playing his guitar to his friends and family near or far.

H ow he loves to go on holiday in his caravan, finding new friends from all around, he's the best in all the town.

U ndoubtedly he is a friendly guy, he is definitely not shy.

A mbitious, adventurous, loyal and fun. Joshua really is an awesome son.

Joshua McClelland (8)
Abbey Primary School, Newtownards

My Happy Place

I'm thinking about my happy place, out on the field that is green
I'm running in my orange top, the same as the rest of my team
I hold my stick and I run with the ball
I practise my skills and score lots of goals
I play in all weather, it doesn't matter at all
I love the sound when the stick hits the ball
I wear two guards to protect my mouth and my shins
I love how the crowd cheers when our team wins
I love scoring goals and that is the reason
My happy place is the hockey season!

Lucy Hutchinson (8)
Abbey Primary School, Newtownards

Dreams Can Come True

W is for wrestling, my favourite thing to watch and play

R is for realising my dreams, a WWE champ I will be one day

E is for energy, something I have a lot of inside of me

S is for strong, I want big muscles for everyone to see

T is for trying my best at everything I do

L is for liking to try things that are new

E is for exciting, what the future holds for me

R is for radical, something I hope to be.

Eli Thompson (8)

Abbey Primary School, Newtownards

This Is Me!

I do tricks and never slip
I am bendy like Wendy

I am happy when I'm at Abbey Primary
I have lots of friends, but I love when I am doing
my bends.

I love to dance and flip around, and never fall to
the ground

With my big sister helping me, she brings out the
best in me.
Without my mum, I wouldn't get much done.
My dad is there for all the fun!

When I dance to the beat I use my feet
I feel powerful, this is my way of life.

Hope Cathcart (8)
Abbey Primary School, Newtownards

The Amazing Eva!

E xcited to learn new things

V ery happy when I spend time with family

A lways up for a challenge

D ashing around the ice rink on a Sunday morning

I magining myself going on scary rides in Florida

M aking new friends at Skerries Caravan Park

O utdoors on my go-kart I come racing down the hill

N oticing how much my schoolwork has improved

D own to the hockey pitch to practise some skills.

Eva Dimond (8)

Abbey Primary School, Newtownards

One Of A Kind

N intendo Switch is my favourite game.

O ut running makes me happy.

A smile on my face you will see.

H aving fun with my friends.

S onic games I love to play.

H oping for a goal in football.

A pizza is my favourite dinner.

N uggets aren't too bad either.

N ight-time reading is the best.

O n the piano you might find me.

N ever stop, full of fun!

Noah Shannon (8)

Abbey Primary School, Newtownards

Emily - Friends Forever

E very morning I wake up and brush my beautiful blonde curly hair for a while with a smile.

M aking my friends and family smile for a while makes my heart flutter with joy I enjoy.

I love helping my brother learn new things, it brings a smile to my face I cannot deny.

L ikeable and hilarious, with a big beaming smile while caring and daring.

Y oung, fun and energetic little girl with a curl.

Emily Kirk (8)

Abbey Primary School, Newtownards

Luke's Daily Routine

Each day I go to school
I learn so much, I'm not a fool.

If I'm good, as my treat
I get my favourite food to eat

I love McDonald's skinny French fries
They are much better than Mum's pork pies.

I play with my laptop after dinner
When I play Roblox, I'm a winner.

In the evening, when Dad nods his head
I look at the clock and it's time for bed.

Luke Shannon (8)
Abbey Primary School, Newtownards

All About Me

A mazing at sports
N ever gives up
D raws excellent artwork
R eading is my favourite
E xpresses a creative mind
W illing to go further and beyond

I am as...
Fast as a cheetah
Determined as a puppy trying to get his toy
Creative as an artist
Happy as Larry when reading my book
Eager as a beaver
Good as gold.

Andrew Le Guiniec (8)
Abbey Primary School, Newtownards

My Super Person

I love this person a lot
But she is a mystery
She has long hair and blue eyes
Who could she be?

She helps me with homework
She makes me yummy food
She always says she loves me
When I'm naughty or good

She keeps me safe and loves me lots
And my sisters and daddy
I am so lucky I live here
With the best family.

Faye Dalziel (8)
Abbey Primary School, Newtownards

All About Darcy

My name is Darcy Millie,
People call me silly.
My favourite horse is Rolo,
He sometimes goes in slow-mo.
I like to play outside,
Rain, hail, snow or shine.
I love animals you bet,
I want to be a vet.
My brother is six foot four,
I couldn't love him more.
My mum and dad are brill,
They really like to chill.

Darcy Lilburn (7)
Abbey Primary School, Newtownards

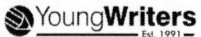

Lucky Layla

T alented and thoughtful
H appy when I am horseriding
I love sweet fruit and crunchy vegetables
S ometimes calm and relaxed

I have a barky dog and two greedy guinea pigs
S chool is so much fun

M y favourite animal is a ferocious lion
E mily is my best friend.

Layla McCoy (8)
Abbey Primary School, Newtownards

This Is Me

T his is me

H ere I am

I love pugs, so cute and fluffy

S ometimes I talk and talk and talk

I am often called a chatterbox

S aturdays are for ju-jitsu which leaves me tired and sleepy

M ost of all I love my mum and dad

E specially when they buy me comics.

Luke Gibson (8)

Abbey Primary School, Newtownards

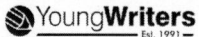

Eva Grace

E njoy zooming on my bike
V ery kind and loving
A dore bunnies, puppies and kittens

G reat at drawing amazing pictures
R olling down hills, racing with Grandad
A lways happy when out in nature
C limbs and swings while at the park
E xcited when I go dancing.

Eva Coffey (8)
Abbey Primary School, Newtownards

My Dream

My name is Codin Hoey.
I am an eight-year-old boy.
When I grow up my dream is to be a YouTuber.
You will watch me from your Switch.
I promise I won't cause a glitch.
Gaming is what I like to do.
Apart from when I change my football shoes.
Liverpool is my team.
Playing football is my dream.

Codin Hoey (8)
Abbey Primary School, Newtownards

My Life In Summer

My name is Tolole and I live in Carrowdore.
I have ducks and chickens and pets galore.
There is lots to do inside,
But summer is nice and warm outside.
I like to play in my pool and stay outside all day long,
If I could I would sleep in it.
I love summer so much.
It makes my year.

Tolole Burnham (8)
Abbey Primary School, Newtownards

All About Me

J umping on the trampoline
A dventurous
C ooking
K ind

M aking people laugh
A lways hungry
G ood at football
I love my family
N ever give up
N ice
E xploring new places
S wimming

Jack Maginnes (8)
Abbey Primary School, Newtownards

About A Boy Called...

C harlie is eight years old

H e's good at football he's been told

A ny sport he'll have a go

R unning, swimming and judo

L earning about places far and near

I nto Cubs with no fear

E njoying everything it is clear.

Charlie Morrow (8)

Abbey Primary School, Newtownards

This Is Me

My name is Charlotte, I have blonde hair and brown eyes
I am caring and funny because I make people laugh
I am also smart and kind and I help people a lot
I am very friendly and I like to make new friends
I am also independent because I can do everything myself.

Charlotte Wilson (8)
Abbey Primary School, Newtownards

Play Time

I like to play all day and night
Football is my fave
I will play until I get it right
And make the perfect save

Another thing I like to do
Is play some racing games
The car I use is royal blue
It sometimes shoots out flames.

Daniel Barritt (8)
Abbey Primary School, Newtownards

The Amazing Madelyn

M agnificent and a monkey
A lways kind to people
D oesn't ever give up
E nergetic and very sporty
L oving and friendly
Y um she says when she eats chocolate
N aturally a talented footballer.

Madelyn Bennett (8)

Abbey Primary School, Newtownards

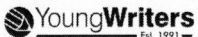

Football

F ootball is the best

O verhead shot

O ver the goal net

T oday I won the match

B all skills

A rchie loves to play football

L et's go to a match

L iverpool is the best team ever.

Bentley Mills Briggs (7)

Abbey Primary School, Newtownards

All About Me

My name is Maxi G!
And I like drinking tea...
Football is my talent
Where I need lots of balance!
In basketball you need to be sturdy
And I would like to be like Steph Curry!
My mum says I'm crazy
But I also like to be lazy!

Max Galbraith (8)
Abbey Primary School, Newtownards

Ourselves

Madeline is energetic, enthusiastic and exciting
My mummy always makes me feel better
Whenever I feel excited my eyes sparkle like
diamonds
I am passionate, caring, helpful and beautiful
But most of all I just enjoy fun, fun, fun.

Madeline Hutton (8)
Abbey Primary School, Newtownards

Teddy Loves Football

I love football, yes I do!
I love football, what about you?
Football brings me lots of joy
I like it better than playing with my toys!
It gives me exercise and keeps me healthy,
When I become a professional it will make me wealthy.

Teddy Jess (8)

Abbey Primary School, Newtownards

The One And Only Will Logan

W illing to help
I maginative brain
L oveable rogue
L ife of the party

L augh a minute
O rdinarily awesome
G roovy mover
A nimal loving
N aturally sporty.

Will Logan (8)

Abbey Primary School, Newtownards

Things About Me

J is for jelly beans I like to eat

A is for 'Adopt Me', my favourite game on Roblox

R is for red, my favourite colour

E is for eyes, mine are blue

D is for the driving range where I play golf.

Jared Scott (8)

Abbey Primary School, Newtownards

Alexis Is...

Alexis is happy like the bright yellow sunflowers.
Alexis is dancing, joyful and light.
Alexis is fun, like a spinning carousel.
Alexis is stylish like an elegant flamingo.
Alexis is an artist, dreaming of being an illustrator.

Alexis Corry (8)
Abbey Primary School, Newtownards

Me

F ast as lightning and the wind
I 'm as smart as a fox
N ever gonna quit trying
L oving my family
E xcited to win the best of the day
Y ellow sun of summer is the best time of year.

Finley O'Neile (8)

Abbey Primary School, Newtownards

This Is Me

My name is Emily, I attend Abbey School
I can't wait to start P5 when I go to the pool

I like to eat Burger King and play with my sister
Lottie
When I'm older I'll have a cat and give it the name
Dotty.

Emily Caughey-Pierce (8)
Abbey Primary School, Newtownards

Who Is She?

She's smart, she's kind
She's made me alive
She's always on the move
Doing everything she can do
She fed me, helped me
She gave me a place to call home
She is my dear beloved mother.

Eva Lowry (8)
Abbey Primary School, Newtownards

Connor's Precious Pizza!

C is for Connor

O nly likes pizza

N ever leaves a slice

N o pineapple, ham, olives for him

O nly pepperoni is his thing

R eady for next time.

Connor Potter (8)

Abbey Primary School, Newtownards

This Is Me, Mollie

This is me
I am Mollie
What makes me happy
Is gymnastics and rugby

I don't like make-up
Or wearing pretty dresses
I love being noisy
And making big messes!

Mollie Mayne (7)
Abbey Primary School, Newtownards

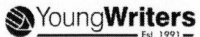

It's All About Me

C assie is my name
A nd I like to play
S weets make me happy all day
S wimming is the best
I am the greatest
E ven though I am only eight.

Cassie Matthews (8)
Abbey Primary School, Newtownards

My Name

T all as tower
A ge is a power
J okes make me laugh
U pset makes me sad
S mart like Google that's why I like noodles.

Tajus Zitkevicius (8)
Abbey Primary School, Newtownards

I'm Not Lyin', I'm Orion

I'm Orion
I'm not lyin'
I'm very good
I love my food
My coat has a hood
I'm never rude
I'm always in a good mood.

Orion Murray (8)
Abbey Primary School, Newtownards

Islay In 5

I ce cream fanatic.

S miling like sunshine.

L over of tail-wagger mutts.

A n island of sunflowers;

Y our shelter.

Islay McCracken (8)

Abbey Primary School, Newtownards

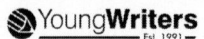

Jack's Amazing Poem

J ack likes to jump around
A pples are Jack's favourite fruit
C oming to eat your chocolate
K nows a lot about animals.

Jack Potter (8)

Abbey Primary School, Newtownards

You'll Pay

C all of Duty, Fortnite and Roblox
O n my Xbox I like to play
D on't disturb me or else...
Y ou will pay!

Cody Stewart (8)
Abbey Primary School, Newtownards

About Birds

Tweet, tweet
I can hear the birds
Tweet, tweet
I can hear their morning song
Tweet, tweet
I hear their bedtime lullaby.

Tillie Orr (8)
Abbey Primary School, Newtownards

Recipe For Me

A dash of fun
A cup of shy
A tablespoon of wild
Chop some laughter in a bowl
And bake for one whole hour.

Beau Drysdale (8)
Abbey Primary School, Newtownards

My Name Is Anna!

A nimal lover amazing

N on-violent, normal

N oble

A bundant love for Jesus.

Anna Magill (8)

Abbey Primary School, Newtownards

Once Upon A Time

O nline school sucked!

N o play when you're at home, just do your work

C lass is back on, back to proper work

E den, my best friend, always has my back

U mbrellas we need when the rainy playtime strike

P ennies you use to pay after school at One-O-One

O n the ball, you must be unless you want to face Mr Kelly

N ow I'm going home to my tutor, it is no rest

A t home, I love to spend time with my family

T his is me, the real me

I smaeel is my name, the best in the world

M y friends and family I love

E nd this poem with a thank you.

Ismaeel Fatawu (9)

Alexandra Parade Primary School, Dennistoun

Skate Your Heart Out!

I like my teacher, she is so kind

C ake I like to bake for you

E lephants, I like them for their floppy ears

S easide is my favourite place to be

K nowledge and trying your best is good for ice skating

A red and pink balloon flew into the sky

T he kindest people are my friends and family

I ce skating is my second favourite sport

N ew York, I really want to go there

G ive a cake to the new neighbour.

Laura Kwiatkowska (9)
Alexandra Parade Primary School, Dennistoun

A Friendly Rhyme

E verything is perfect, even you
R ude is bad, don't be bad
I try my best every day
N ever let your family or your friends down

M ums are for loving, helping and caring
U nder the sun is a bright place to hide
R avens are the best so be a Ravenclaw
R ainy days are bad but not when I'm with my family
A day is good when I'm with my family
Y ou're a sunflower!

Erin Murray (9)
Alexandra Parade Primary School, Dennistoun

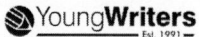

Shine And Skate

R ollerskating is my hobby

O h, of course, I skate every day

L augh with my friends forever

L eave it all and skate away

E ncourage how to skate, such a glorious way

R emarkable, such a remarkable sport

S weet sun, shine, shine, shine

K arcyn is my name

A nd how I admire skating so much

T alent you need to skate

E xciting so it is, you know how it is!

Karcyn Guest (9)

Alexandra Parade Primary School, Dennistoun

Basketball

B ounce the ball, shoot in the hoop
A fantastic game on the court
S hoot from the three-pointer
K eep the ball away from the other players
E veryone come and watch the NBA play
T ickets are VIP for the special people in my life
B lock the ball from the hoop
A good time on the court
L ower the ball under your hip
L ike the players you play with.

Abynabi Gebremariam (9)

Alexandra Parade Primary School, Dennistoun

Minecraft

M inecraft is the best game you will ever know

I ce in Minecraft is kinda slippery

N ether portal is where you can fight the gasp and the

E nder dragon to build stuff you need

C obblestones to build a minecart you need

R ails, you have to kill the zombies

A nd spiders, you will have so much

F un in Minecraft

T ime changes in Minecraft, day to night.

Aarav Gundle (9)

Alexandra Parade Primary School, Dennistoun

This Is Me

M usic is a pattern of sounds by people singing or playing instruments

U nable to play a couple of instruments like a violin

S ing a song, you make music with your voice

I can play a few instruments like drums and guitar

C an sing a couple of different ways

I 'm really good at playing the drums

A nd I'm amazing at guitar as well

N early a musician.

Charlie McDonald (9)

Alexandra Parade Primary School, Dennistoun

This Is Jessica

J am doughnuts are my favourite
E verything on YouTube is so good
S weets are so good that I could go to sleep
S lime is so cool because you can get so many
I ce cream, I could eat all day
C ake, I can post a TikTok of
A pretty unicorn will make you happy.

Jessica Jameson (9)
Alexandra Parade Primary School, Dennistoun

Murawski

M y life is good because I love my family
U mbrellas are good for stopping the rain
R unning I am very good at
A lex is my dad
W ater is fresh
S peed is the key
K ing bees are big
I ce is cold because it is made of water.

Loui Murawski (10)

Alexandra Parade Primary School, Dennistoun

Meme

M emes make you laugh
E ntertain you and make you smile
M itchell memes, do not touch
E ven if you copy memes, they won't be funny.

Mitchell Beattie (9)

Alexandra Parade Primary School, Dennistoun

Clyde

C lyde is a good name
L ogan is my brother
Y aks I like
D eborah is my auntie
E very day, I try to put a smile on my face.

Clyde Campbell (9)

Alexandra Parade Primary School, Dennistoun

This Is Me

Hello! My name is Amelia
I play a lot with Julia
But I like playing with family more
Would you like a tour?
My dream job is a scientist/inventor
Or maybe a doctor or artist is better
My two favourite people in the world are my
mummy and sister
No one is better, mister
My feelings have a disco when they're happy
I like sticks, they're never too tacky
I'm really silly and I love animals, they're so fluffy
Not all of them are fluffy, some are scruffy
I still like animals though I also like bucket hats!
My sister bought me one (I think my Mummy's
getting me one)
And I'm never letting it go gone
I ask a lot of questions
I'm also bad at rhyming
So my suggestion?
I like playing on my devices with family and at the
park!

Me and my friends play games where we pretend
to bark
So I'm trained to bark at people who upset my
family
My hands are dead so goodbye!

Amelia Gajewska (8)

Bearbrook Combined School, Aylesbury

This Is Me!

T alking is what I do most of the time to friends, family and others.

H elping my family is my job. If my family is not happy I try to help.

I like the colour blue because it reminds me of the ocean waves.

S tories are my favourite because when I need them I go into my own world.

I love my family because without them I wouldn't be happy.

S aying funny things to my friends to make them smile.

M y pets are special and important and they're very fun to play with.

E nchanted games are magical to me because when I play them I think of good ideas.

Julia Kwiecinska (8)

Bearbrook Combined School, Aylesbury

This Is Me

This is me
How I act
I'm one of a kind inside and out
Samples of what I like makes me me.

I'm my own person
Seasons make me wear the same clothes as other people
But it doesn't change who I am on the inside.

Moments when I fail I get back up again
And say never give up on your dreams
And never stop being you.

Ears open, I say it's easy to be me
And always believe in yourself and your dreams
Because soon you will achieve them.

Ariella Olalekan (8)
Bearbrook Combined School, Aylesbury

All About Me

I'm as funny as a cat, as kind as the world.
I love VW cars.
I like going camping to watch the stars.
I like being taught by Miss Smith and friends.
My family encourages me to be what I want to be.
I want to control a Beetle that looks rusty.
I want to work in the Air Force like others.
I love thesauruses because they are important to me.
I love myself because I am myself.
When I'm not happy the only thing that gets me happy is my dad.

Noah Saunders (8)
Bearbrook Combined School, Aylesbury

This Is Me!

T hea is my name and I like it

H alloween is my least favourite time of the year, it's scary

I love animals a lot and I'm as fast as a car

S lime is really really fun to play with to me

I am kind and loving with a lovely family

S wimming is fun and I try my best

M iss Smith is the best teacher, she's as funny as a clown

E louise is my cousin and she's the best person.

Thea Beales (7)

Bearbrook Combined School, Aylesbury

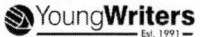
This Is Me!

T heo is my name and sometimes I'm a hot head

H appiness grows inside me every day, even in bed

I t's my dream to be a football legend

S ome days I go out and smash the ball in

I find everything in school so cool and fascinating

S ometimes I go into my own world

M y family love me above and beyond

E ven they believe in me to accomplish anything.

Theo Neophytou (8)

Bearbrook Combined School, Aylesbury

This Is Me

T rue gymnastics pro
H ate tomatoes in any type of way
I dislike onions, they're as white as snow
S ongs are my jam, I dance every day

I am as fast as a jaguar running at max speed
S inging is my favourite thing

M ichael Morpurgo is my favourite author
E leventh of November is my birthday.

Ashton Forchione (8)
Bearbrook Combined School, Aylesbury

My Life

Chaos in my flat
At least we don't have bats
My parents are the best
Better than all the rest

My friends are the greatest
We are always the latest
I eat lollipops, they are yummy
They make me have a happy tummy

I have brown eyes like a tree stalk
And I like to talk
I love myself and everyone else.

Gabriella Ehujor (8)
Bearbrook Combined School, Aylesbury

Someone I Love

Lies on me when I am sad
Plays with me and drives Mum mad!
Bounces from side to side
Sleeps in Mum's bed and likes to hide
Chewbacca is the way he talks
Takes off like a Lamborghini instead of walking
Licks me all the time
I'm glad we rescued him and that he's mine.

Answer: My dog.

Alexis-Mae Peck (8)
Bearbrook Combined School, Aylesbury

This Is Me!

I like Roblox because it's fun
I like cupcakes and eat every one!
I like sour snake sweets which make my face
scrunch up
But ice skating is my favourite treat
I love gymnastics with silk ribbons
Thankfully no one sounds like a gibbon
My favourite subject at school is PE
I love school and being me.

Harper Morris (8)
Bearbrook Combined School, Aylesbury

This Is Me

I like to play Roblox because it's great.
I like cupcakes and I clean the plate.
I like make-up because I look fancy.
I am as fast as a cheetah but not a Lamborghini.
I like SSSniperWolf and am a bit teeny.
I like how I have my own library of books to read.
Toast and macaroni are things I like to cook.

Iris Correia (8)

Bearbrook Combined School, Aylesbury

Gamers

G ames online are my favourite things to play

A ll games are amazing like Fortnite and Roblox

M inecraft too, I think games are the best

E ven songs about games will make you curious

R acing car games I play when the sun is bright

S ometimes I play games at night.

Josiah Joseph (8)
Bearbrook Combined School, Aylesbury

This Is Me

T he school that I go to is the best
H appy with anything I do
I love maths
S chool is my life

I like literacy but I need to improve
S chool is important

M y favourite sport is basketball
E ven if I don't catch the ball.

Junior Makombe (8)
Bearbrook Combined School, Aylesbury

This Is Him

He makes me laugh and he is as skinny as a dot
He loves magic and tricks me a lot
He always has a smile on his face
He drives me mad when we are playing chase
When I am nervous he is so curious
He is as fierce as a tiger
And as tough as a lion
He makes me happy a lot of the time.

Tyler Burkhill (8)
Bearbrook Combined School, Aylesbury

This Is Me

I am a massive animal lover.
I am like a goldfish at swimming.
My dream job is a marine ecologist.
I am a reading rabbit, it is a very fun habit.
I am a hater of loud sounds.
I am as frightened as a hamster of spiders.
I get a bit moody when I do maths
But I am a dividing diva.

Isabel Booth (7)

Bearbrook Combined School, Aylesbury

This Is Me!

I'm amazing at art.
I'm as fast as a tiger.
I'm as sneaky as a spider.
I'm as long as a table.
I'm amazing at games.
My ADHD can be a label.
Sometimes I get the blame
But chatting makes me feel calm and free.
I am unique and I love being me!

Terry Breese-Ellis (8)
Bearbrook Combined School, Aylesbury

All About Me

I have brown eyes and the same coloured hair
I love having friends and showing I care

I have a blended family as my parents separated
I like having two homes but I get frustrated

I love drawing pictures for my family
Making them happy

This is me!

Olivia Sheen (8)
Bearbrook Combined School, Aylesbury

All About Football!

My favourite footballer is the best
He's more skilled than the rest
He's as strong as The Hulk and tall like a tree
He likes telling jokes which are really funny
When I grow up I want to be a famous footballer.
Who is he?

Answer: C Ronaldo.

Muhammad Usayd Ali (8)

Bearbrook Combined School, Aylesbury

This Is Me

I am caring, loving and kind.
I like animals, my favourite is a dog called Poppy.
I like super shiny things.
I like school.
I love my long blonde hair like a princess'.
I love my best friend and family.
My smile makes me special and I share it with everyone.

Caroline Norman (7)
Bearbrook Combined School, Aylesbury

This Is Me

I have black hair like a spider
I have grey eyes like an elephant
I am a good gamer
I am the best at football in the class
I am the best at riding fast on my bike
My daddy is my favourite person
He makes me happy every day
And I give him lots of hugs.

Dayyan Shakeel (8)
Bearbrook Combined School, Aylesbury

What Am I?

I swim through the ocean at nearly 800 metres deep.
I am protected by a hard house.
I weave through the kelp, but I never move my torso.
I devour jellyfish for every dish.
I am as green as grass.
What am I?

Answer: A turtle.

Finley Newbery (8)
Bearbrook Combined School, Aylesbury

This Is Me

My eyes are as brown as the branches.
I take care of people.
I love to play Roblox, I play it with my friends.
I am kind, smart, strong and have good writing.
I never give up on things.
I am as sweet as cake.
I also like to bake.

Georgina Owusu Tabiri (7)
Bearbrook Combined School, Aylesbury

I Am

I love football because it is my favourite sport.
I am good at maths and I know all my times tables.
I love running and I am as fast as a tiger.
I can draw like Yayoi Kusama.
I love to laugh and joke.
It's fun to do with a poke.

Al-Rayaan Khan (8)
Bearbrook Combined School, Aylesbury

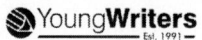

What Am I?

I wear a big coat of fur to keep me warm,
I stay with my mum because I'm too young,
Some people call me cute and cuddly,
And I live in the forest but also in the zoo.
What am I?

Answer: A baby wolf.

Andrew van der Merwe (8)
Bearbrook Combined School, Aylesbury

My Favourite Thing

I glow bright when I turn on
When the person's gone I rest
People play on me for far too long
When people lose they scream
I wish they would work as a team.
What am I?

Answer: A PlayStation 5.

Heath McCracken (8)
Bearbrook Combined School, Aylesbury

This Is Me

My hair is like the dark night
I have brown eyes like a bear
I am the best at gaming
I am as fast as a lion
I am a superstar at Roblox
I love playing Minecraft
I am going to be a Minecraft master.

Maria Bibi (7)
Bearbrook Combined School, Aylesbury

Who Is He?

He is as strong as a tiger
He is as sleepy as a sloth
He is as tall as an elephant
He is as thin as a giraffe's neck
He is as talented as an artist.
Who is he?

Answer: My dad!

Finley Seymour (8)
Bearbrook Combined School, Aylesbury

I Am A...

Fast runner like a cheetah
I am calm, caring and kind
I am an artist who loves to draw things
I am helpful and loving
I am tall as a tree
I am a banana eater like a sneaky monkey.

Manha Moazzam (8)
Bearbrook Combined School, Aylesbury

All About Me

I have blonde hair
I have azure eyes like the sea
I am very good at streaming
I am a superstar at Minecraft
I am as kind as my daddy
I am as fast as Sonic
I run all day!

Carter Leone (8)
Bearbrook Combined School, Aylesbury

My Favourite Animal

I live in a house
I am as soft as a teddy bear
I have pointy ears
I chase mice
I am usually nice
I'm a furry feline.
What am I?

Answer: A cat.

Charlie Ladbrooke (8)
Bearbrook Combined School, Aylesbury

Riddle

I live in a house
I am as loud as an elephant
I have a black tail
I have a good sense of smell
I bark when I hear a bell.
What am I?

Answer: A dog.

Theo Jeeves (8)
Bearbrook Combined School, Aylesbury

What Am I?

I live in a forest
I start as green as a grasshopper
But I can change colour
I can stick my tongue 20cm out
What am I?

Answer: A chameleon.

Aamari Esimaje (7)
Bearbrook Combined School, Aylesbury

I Am...

I am a bike rider
I am a candy eater
I am patient, playful and private
I am a helper and clean my house
I am sometimes quiet like a mouse.

Maira Basharat (8)
Bearbrook Combined School, Aylesbury

This Is Me

I am a footballer
I am as fast as a cheetah
I am a basketball player
I am a helper
I am a good person
I am kind, caring and calm.

Bilal Khazeem (8)
Bearbrook Combined School, Aylesbury

About Me

I am tall like a dinosaur
I like to ride my bike
I help Mum with the chores
Playing at the park is what I like
This is me!

Mariaa Khalil (8)

Bearbrook Combined School, Aylesbury

All About Me

I am kind, caring and calm
I am as fast as a dolphin
I am a swimmer
I am a gamer
I am an ice cream lover
This is me.

Gavin Carcedo (8)
Bearbrook Combined School, Aylesbury

Me!

I am a footballer
I am nice
I am a gamer
I am fast, fun and funky
I am as speedy as a Lamborghini.

Alfie Walker (8)
Bearbrook Combined School, Aylesbury

All About Me

I am a footballer
I am a gamer
I am lovely
I am kind, caring and clean.

Joey Thirkettle (8)
Bearbrook Combined School, Aylesbury

Inspiring Individual

K aiya, she's a dragon person

A girl from a wonderful world

I love a singer from the highlands

Y ou think it's a whole new world

A nime is my thing, Japanese fashion is like ping!

M y books are full of mystery, they're all about dragons

O nly one who likes Nati Dreddd, a singer, I listen to all her songs in my free time

W onderful drawings I adore to do, bunnies, ninjas, I draw them too!

A nd all my dream places to go, Japan, Scotland, and San Diego

T o go along my favourite path, the one that leads me to my heart

I n my imagination, I run wild just so freely, it's the best part

S o follow me along the mystical path of glory

M y imagination runs wild and free, making up stories of magic and art

E nd the day drawing, anime, Erza Scarlet from Dragon Cry? I love it all!

Kaiya Andrew-Mowat (10)
Carnalridge Primary School, Portrush

My Bee And Me

The other day I saw a bee
On the sandy beach by the sea
It was a very strange bee, it was very kind
It was probably the strangest you can find!
Black and yellow was its natural colour
So you can definitely find another!
I named the bee Rose
But when I went into the sea I froze.
I ran back to the shore
But on the sand I felt something sore
It was a shell in my foot that hurt a lot
I took it out and there I thought
I should open a seashell shop!
It took a while to prepare
But then on the news I heard about a bear
The bear was eating nothing other than bees!
So I got Rose and headed to the seas
We sailed to New York, the big city
And I opened my shop there and there was no pity
We sold some more shells today
But then there was a big delay

There must have been a theft
There were no shells left
I went to get some shells but there were none
But we had a good day and that was fun.
I said to Rose, "You will always be my best friend
Until the very end."

Maya Kelly (10)
Carnalridge Primary School, Portrush

Banana

My name is Hannah Banana
I moved here from Montana
I am nine years old
I am brave and bold

I am very funny
My favourite animal is a bunny
I am also really good fun
I read when my work is done

My favourite subject is art
In which I'm really smart
And all the time I really need
To read, read, read

My friend, Isaiah, I miss a lot
But he lives in Arizona where it's hot, hot, hot
Before I moved here I lived in a flat
And I've never had a pet like a dog or a cat

I love to ski
And drink bubble tea

I'm not tall or long
But still I stay strong

Before this year I've never been to school
And I think that that's really cool
My favourite colours are purple and teal
And happy is the emotion I love to feel.

Hannah McCormick (9)
Carnalridge Primary School, Portrush

My Life

R unning down the pitch
U sing all the space
G oing into a ruck
B uying kits and scrum hats
Y elling at each other in the rain

M arvellous Mum
U ses everything
M ade of money

D ad is the best
A lso very brave
D ad looks after me

T aylors potatoes
R otten potatoes in the bin
A lexander's ride
C urious how it works
T ato maker
O bviously the best
R unning through the fields

F an of farming
A lexander feeds the calves
R unning after herds
M aking milk
I magining what town life is like
N ever giving up
G oing everywhere.

Alexander Taylor (10)

Carnalridge Primary School, Portrush

Life So Far

I play for Ballymoney Rugby Club
I am a forward and am never a sub
When I'm injured I watch rugby in the hub
When I watch Ireland they always get the dub

I am a centre back
My football kit is black
The other defender is called Jack
Sometimes I go up and attack

My dad works on the farm
My mom does me no harm
My brother always turns on the fire alarm
My sister likes to say the word, "Darn!"

Luis Díaz is our best player
Orige is a betrayer
Virgil van Dijk is a slayer
Luis Díaz wears a lot of layers

My name is Alastair Campbell
I have a cousin called Randell

I broke my door handle
I have a big candle.

Alastair Campbell (10)
Carnalridge Primary School, Portrush

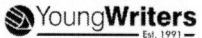

Me, Myself And I

I am a messy ten-year-old,
I find myself brave and bold.
I love going to the sunny seashore,
And I hate doing boring chores!
People say I am quite funny,
I adore cute animals like fluffy bunnies!
My friends are super duper fun,
I love baking delicious chocolate buns,
My personality is fun and cool,
Even though sometimes I may act like a fool!
Music is my thing,
To laugh, to dance, to sing,
I wish to become a famous singer and actor,
And win the X Factor!
My family is full with love and laughter,
Getting better each chapter.
So this is me,
And who I'm meant to be!

Julia Fornara (10)
Carnalridge Primary School, Portrush

All About Me

I'm kind and caring,
Always sharing,
My fave thing is unicorns
And I do not like thorns.

My friends are loving and weird,
But sometimes their heads get a bit cleared,
Oh, they're bold and fearless,
But sometimes they are cheerless.

Oh, that lovely sport,
And where I play is a tennis court,
Swimming is my absolute favourite,
I love it because of the nice soothing swimming
pool.

My fave food is parma ham,
But I really hate the taste of jam,
Some people think I'm weird for liking blue cheese,
And I like the apples that fall from trees.

Catherine Rainey (10)
Carnalridge Primary School, Portrush

Sporty, Snoopy, Smart Sarah The Sea Life Explorer

Stare as she awakens,
Not to her satisfaction,
Her intelligent brain curious as ever
Charged up and ready for action!

A crazy fun day ahead of her,
Full sports and Irish dancing too,
Hockey, tennis and surfing,
Over the ocean blue.

After all the excitement,
She does lots of Minecraft or Lego,
On an adventure with reading,
On a journey with flute and piano.

Finally back to bed!
And maybe you will find,
Baby turtles clumsily,
Swimming across my mind.

Sarah McCaughey (10)
Carnalridge Primary School, Portrush

Everything About Me

I'm a pretty messy girl,
But my life is sometimes in a whirl.

My favourite subject is maths,
And in netball all you only hear is "Pass!"

All my friends say I'm awesome,
But sometimes I feel like a possum!

All my friends say I'm really fun,
In my Irish dancing I always like to get number
one.

I am really passionate,
But my parents are always saying we need to
ration it.

I think I'm pretty cool,
And I love to swim in the pool.

Daisy Ridley Anderson (10)
Carnalridge Primary School, Portrush

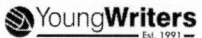
Rio

R onaldo is my favourite football player
I love to play football and many other sports
O bviously I am the best

M arvellous me
C ool style
D eadly at football
O utrageously skilful
N ominated for the school football team
A ccurate shooting
L ong shots
D umb things.

Rio McDonald (10)

Carnalridge Primary School, Portrush

Me

My favourite sport is swimming
And I love winning
When I ride a horse
I zoom around the course

I am smart and kind
A more true and honest friend you cannot find
My favourite subject is maths
I love taking baths.

Amelia McCaughern (10)
Carnalridge Primary School, Portrush

The Things That Make Me, Me!

Everyone around me thinks I'm fun, bubbly
and nice
Intelligent, good-looking and ever so bright
And while I agree with them
There's so much more to see
So here is the truth
On what I think about me

I want to be
A zoologist when I'm older
When I am much brighter
And when I'm much bolder
This is because
I love all living things
For example, I love birds
They make me want to sing

I also like scientific things
And sensible thinking
All these scientific ideas

Are ever so interesting
I love science so much
That in school they made me
A science ambassador
For all to see

I love to read books
Oh, yes I do
I even read
As I put on my shoe
The words take me away
Into another world
Where magic is real
For every boy and girl

I don't know if you knew
But I'm a British Pakistani
And in my house
We like to eat biryani

Whenever I visit Pakistan
I always go to the beach
I love the hot weather
And the splashing sea

Now I have told you
A few things about me
From my love for science
To the fact I love to read
I hope you've understood
My personality
Because these are the things
That make me, me!

Eshaal Fatima Merchant (9)

Hampton Hargate Primary School, Hampton Hargate

Every Time I Go...

Every time I go to school, I see an amazing teacher
Every time I go home, I get cared for and loved by
my family
Every time I go outside, I feel a small breeze
Every time I go to bed, I see a dream in my head
Every time I go on my Xbox, I play with my sister
Every time I see my brother, he always wants to
play with me
Every time I go to stroke one of my cats, they feel
so soft.

I love my super cute brother and sister
I love my mum and dad
I love my cats; Zeus, Dusty and Kobi
I love my family in London
I love my cousins
I love my aunties
I love my nan and nana.

Alexa Abbott-New (8)
Hampton Hargate Primary School, Hampton Hargate

Birthday!

Everybody waits for this one day
Which is, of course, your birthday.
So excited
Everyone invited!

Jumping happily
With your friends and family.
Can't believe the day has come,
Waiting and waiting, chewing your gum.

Birthday gifts all over the room,
And one of them might be a broom.
At the end, you're really tired,
It's like you have just been fired.

We come to an end,
When you just pretend
That you're not sleepy,
But you look creepy!

So now we wait another year,
Which is actually really near,

Which feels like it's a long time
Oh sorry, gotta go, it's bedtime

So now I have to go to sleep,
Wake me up
When you hear a creak...

Felicity Joe (9)
Hampton Hargate Primary School, Hampton Hargate

All About Me

This is a poem that's all about me
From the top of my head to the tips of my toes
I'm funny, happy, helpful and kind
I don't have a favourite colour
I just can't make up my mind
I really love school, family and friends
I love reading books right to the very end
I'm flexible, friendly and cheerful
I'm really glad
I love painting and drawing pictures on my giant art pad
I eat chicken dippers all day long, I just couldn't stop
I like big juicy strawberries with ice cream on top.

Annalise Edwards (8)
Hampton Hargate Primary School, Hampton Hargate

This Is Me

I am a living testimony
Leaving within those that are
blessed to witness my inspiring journey.

I was born chubby but healthy
My parents said I had some developmental
delays however I am grateful to have touched
lives positively with my story
With God, I achieve my goals at my own pace
and time.

I stammer but it doesn't stop me from talking
I love my family because they love me too
I love computers but I am not perfect yet
I am a happy boy because God is with me.

Kaobim Anajekwu (8)
Hampton Hargate Primary School, Hampton Hargate

Imaginary Land

Pink, blue and bright green
Some people are not so keen
Always happy, never sad
When you're at Imaginary Land
Not tired and feeling awake
After you've ridden the water snake
I never like people sad
Because I'm the owner of Imaginary Land
The grass is so green and the trees so tall
Some people don't take care of their gardens at all
So come to Imaginary Land, you won't regret it
Because you'll love the sandpit!

Maddison Beeke (9)
Hampton Hargate Primary School, Hampton Hargate

Chicken Wing!

C heerfully role-playing with my bestie, Nadia
H ufflepuff is my house
I ngenious jokes
C ucumber presents for my friend, Amber
K eira is my sister's name
E ve is what I reply to
N adia always has a smile

W inning poem contests is my game
I nvolving Tracy Beaker in my life is key
N oisy when I sleep (snoring)
G randpa T giving me 50ps when I need them the most.

Eve Taylor (9)
Hampton Hargate Primary School, Hampton Hargate

I Wonder Why

I wonder why birds fly
They catch my eye
I wonder why the sky is blue
Maybe clouds stick with glue
I wonder why I can ride my bike so fast
So I can reach school in a blast
I wonder how I can do flips on a trampoline
I don't have to wait until I'm thirteen
I have a set routine
And I love different cuisine
I love my family so much
Because they're as sweet as fudge
I wonder what, how, and why
So I can comply.

Muhammad Rayyan Siddiqi (9)
Hampton Hargate Primary School, Hampton Hargate

Place In My Heart

There is a place in my heart
It has millions of spaces
Nothing can break this giant heart
Not even when I'm sad
You all have a place in my heart
In my kind, generous heart
When I'm down you help me up again
You make me happy when you're around
Anyone makes me happy when they're around
Nothing can break my heart
My kind, generous heart
There is a place in my heart for everyone
There is a place in my heart.

Hailie Chilman (9)
Hampton Hargate Primary School, Hampton Hargate

Man Of The Moment!

R unning down the wing as fast as a cheetah

O ver the ball I step, defenders I'll beat ya

N obody can beat us, my team is the best

A t the end of the day, I like a good rest

L eading United's attack at Old Trafford, the Theatre of Dreams

D estroying defenders, tearing them apart at the seams

O f all the world's players, the greatest goal scorer ever seen!

William Liddle (9)

Hampton Hargate Primary School, Hampton Hargate

Me

The other country I came from
It was a lovely summer
My age that time was only four
I travelled with my mother

No words in English, I would know
But started school that year
Reading, phonics, maths and so
I learn to speak and hear

I've just had a birthday and I'm nine
At school, I have some friends and fun
Enjoy my life and family time
My best friend is my mum.

Tymoteusz Sietnik (9)
Hampton Hargate Primary School, Hampton Hargate

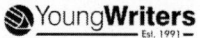
Emotions

Emotions are something in you
You might even feel blue
You are probably happy
Or maybe flappy
You could feel excited
You watched, as the boxers fighted
You can feel worried
The cat jumped as quick as a kangaroo
Because it hurried
Also, you can be scared
Because you cared
You might feel mad
Because you are sad
But now I feel glad
I am not sad
And I'm not mad.

Haasika Vishnuprabhu (9)
Hampton Hargate Primary School, Hampton Hargate

This Is About Me

One of my favourite things is Minnie Mouse
All day long wearing a blouse
I also really like Dobby
Who's back in the lobby
My favourite place is Costa
Driving in my mum's Corsa
The wonderful world of space
Watching my new kittens chase
Cuddling my teddies
Eating berries
I love Baby Yoda
Doing my daily yoga
Oh, have you seen Hulk?
With his luck
Which I love.

Maisie Walthew (8)

Hampton Hargate Primary School, Hampton Hargate

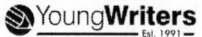

This Is Me

T hings that I love are books and cute cats
H owever, do they hunt? They're as silent as a rat
I nterestingly, I like the peace and quiet
S itting in the sun and looking at violets

I nside I love to make lots of crafts
S mall trees, houses and even rafts

M aybe if I'm feeling happy
E ven I might play with Abbey!

Nishta Bhatia (9)
Hampton Hargate Primary School, Hampton Hargate

Lois

They are funny and silly and they make Daddy
laugh
They have a mum who likes lilies and taking a long
hot bath
Two sisters who always are so annoying, it makes
them scream... argh!
They never stop, no never stop, so they annoy
them back, haha!
They are the youngest of the three, the baby of the
family
Who is 'they'? I hear you ask
Why it's Lois and she's full of sass!

Lois Cook (9)
Hampton Hargate Primary School, Hampton Hargate

All About Me

I am Lara and I like the colour pink
While I climb my special tree and think

I like doing gymnastics
And I sort of like mathematics

My best friend is Harriet
As a team we could be called 'Larriet'
(Lara and Harriet makes Larriet)

I like playing outside
You'll find me walking, talking
And jumping on my trampoline.

Lara Wilkins (9)
Hampton Hargate Primary School, Hampton Hargate

My Animal

Sleepy like a koala
Soft like a lion's mane
Lazy like a sloth
Purring like a rattle full of soft beads shaking
Kind and cuddly like a teddy bear
I love to feed you in the morning
And you are always there when I get home from school
You are super special to me, your cuddles are the best
When I am upset, you make me feel a lot better.

Niamh Jones (9)
Hampton Hargate Primary School, Hampton Hargate

The Best Way To Describe Me

Always with a smile, always liking my style
As fast as a cheetah winning all races by a metre
As smart as a chimpanzee, I can even outsmart bees
I never say no to myself, even when it's hard and I know
I resist my pain because of my brain
I'm grateful and helpful and cheerful for others
These are the things that always describe me.

Gabriel Nimakoh (9)
Hampton Hargate Primary School, Hampton Hargate

All About Me!

I have a mind full of math,
I think of numbers while in the bath.

Playing with my brother is so much fun,
Sometimes I feel we are two in one.

My mom says I am kind and caring,
While my dad says I should be strong and daring.

I want to explore all the continents of Earth,
Starting with Greenland down to Perth.

Sauvik Srivastava (9)
Hampton Hargate Primary School, Hampton Hargate

This Is Me

D avid is my name
A nd I always like to play
V ery happy, kind and polite
I s something that can be described
D avid is funny and great

B eing a dentist is wistfully his fate
E very one of his friends like him
L oves to play football
U ltimately, this is me.

David Marian Belu (9)
Hampton Hargate Primary School, Hampton Hargate

This Is Me

The best thing about me is that
I am the sun shining brightly
I am the moon moving mountains
I am the ocean blue, bold and brilliant
I am the stars twinkling in your heart
I am the wind whispering in your ears
I am a tree, strong and steel-like
I am my mummy
I am my daddy
I am like you and you are like me.

Joshua Lorde (8)
Hampton Hargate Primary School, Hampton Hargate

Space

Space, a cool and interesting place
Sadly, aliens can't solve this case
Planets and dwarves as far as the eye can see
Only one planet will survive
I wonder which it will be

As light as the sun beams
I look less sad as it might seem

As the stars glare down
They see everyone in this town.

Tulula Rushmer (9)
Hampton Hargate Primary School, Hampton Hargate

Sprint

S printing is something I love to do
P eople all around the world love it too
R unning ahead as fast as the speed of light
I speed across like a shooting star in the night
N ot all people can run super-fast but that's okay
T ogether we sprint ahead in our own way.

Ria Azar (9)

Hampton Hargate Primary School, Hampton Hargate

Back Of The Net

I woke up as excited as a puppy
Today is Sunday
A day full of sun
I went outside
And started to kick the ball around
I watched the ball roll around
Like a tumbleweed in the dry desert
I kicked the ball in the white net
With such power...
I made a hole
In the back of the net!

Albert Gabroveanu (9)
Hampton Hargate Primary School, Hampton Hargate

All About Me

I like to eat food
And I am always in a good mood
I like the moon
Just like the raccoon
I am good at art
But I get messy
I have friends
Because I can blend
I have a brother
And a great mother
I like llamas
With lots of colours
I like Fridays
But not Mondays.

Amber Louise Lemmon (9)
Hampton Hargate Primary School, Hampton Hargate

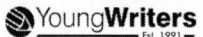

I Am Unique

J umping and prancing with glee
O bservant of what she sees amongst herself
A nimals and insects flutter and crawl
N ever been left out or forgotten
N ever been unkept with less love
A nd all you need to know is that I'm unique in every single way.

Joanna Akintola (9)
Hampton Hargate Primary School, Hampton Hargate

Me And Football

F or me, football is important
O f course, I love it
O r dodgeball, either one
T eamwork helps me
B ut I do love rounders too
A nd maybe could be famous
L ike all my friends I like football
L ove and laughter are my favourite.

Harriet Lawrence (8)
Hampton Hargate Primary School, Hampton Hargate

All About Me

My name is Lucas
I like football
I am so good
But it is raining so I need a hood
I am too good
I like drawing
It's not boring
I like flamingoes
They are so pink
They wink at me
I like sweets
When they're sour
I'll eat them every hour.

Lucas Peters (9)
Hampton Hargate Primary School, Hampton Hargate

Liam King

L iam
I like life
A n artist is my dream
M aking animations with a team

K icking a football is fun
I n the sun is the part of the fun
N ice friends are exciting
G oing to my friend's house is exciting.

Liam King (9)
Hampton Hargate Primary School, Hampton Hargate

The Child Of Spring

I was born in spring
When cherry trees look like they are covered in
snow
Blossoming flowers are as colourful as the rainbow
Birds are gathering and tweeting like a choir
Because they have arrived for the celebration of
spring
I am Emīlija, the child of spring.

Emīlija Millere (8)
Hampton Hargate Primary School, Hampton Hargate

This Is Me

I might not be the most intelligent but I'm the most creative
I'm good at building Lego
I can run long distances
I can walk long distances
I can draw anything
I'm happy playing with my friends
Orange is my colour
I'm a smiley boy.

Leonardo Kakosch (9)

Hampton Hargate Primary School, Hampton Hargate

Crazy Kayde

I'm a boy with brown hair and brown eyes
I know my animals
Especially reptiles

I have two sisters and one cat
And sometimes I can act like a brat

When it's dark at night
My favourite thing is to play Fortnite.

Kayde Di Gorno (8)
Hampton Hargate Primary School, Hampton Hargate

This Is Me

My name is Maeva Mitchell
I live in Hampton Hargate
I am the TikTok queen
And I'm not even a teen
I like to dance and sing
I wear lots of bling
I am always happy and jolly
But not when it rains
I need my brolly!

Maeva Mitchell (9)
Hampton Hargate Primary School, Hampton Hargate

My New Day

I wake up with a smile
And have books in a pile

Get dressed in a quick
Then make a new trick

Go downstairs to get a drink
After go and colour using pink

Go to school and repeat
Go home and sleep.

Renee Jarvis (9)
Hampton Hargate Primary School, Hampton Hargate

All About Me

My name is Megan and I like green
I'm sweet like sugar
With the biggest smile you've ever seen
I'm as funny as a monkey
And also kind and funky
I'm as happy as a little girl can be.

Megan Colbert (9)
Hampton Hargate Primary School, Hampton Hargate

Riyah

R ainbows are as colourful as my eyes
I magination flows through my brain
Y ellow sun is no match for my brightness
A rtistic as a flower
H oney is as sweet as my heart.

Riyah Valani (9)
Hampton Hargate Primary School, Hampton Hargate

Me

There are many things that make me, me
I'm short, happy and sad but mostly happy
I hate beans, I like spaghetti and sausages
I like to ride my scooter
And don't like to be told what to do.

Lydia Pattison (8)
Hampton Hargate Primary School, Hampton Hargate

Rain

I can see raindrops falling down the trees
I can feel the air going through the trees
The smell of the grass after the rain puts me at
ease
The crunch of dry leaves makes my heart rate
increase.

Hassan Shiraz (9)
Hampton Hargate Primary School, Hampton Hargate

All About Everton

E verton

V ery good team

E xcited when they win vs Liverpool

R icharlison

T ownsend

O n Everton's side

N o one will beat them.

Anna Donovan (9)

Hampton Hargate Primary School, Hampton Hargate

The Sleepover

One time it was Ramadan
And our friends came over for iftar
We hid the bags
So no one would know
We had a good time with our friends over
But now it was time for the sleepover!

Zainab Naqvi (8)
Hampton Hargate Primary School, Hampton Hargate

Me!

A ysha is my name

Y es, my favourite animal is a horse

S o, my favourite snack is yoghurt

H olidays are my favourite

A eroplane rides are scary.

Aysha Choudhry (9)

Hampton Hargate Primary School, Hampton Hargate

Kick

My name is Louie
I like to kick
When I play football
I do tricks
I have so many moves
It's hard to pick
I like to kick in karate
And then do a backflip!

Louie Hawksford (9)
Hampton Hargate Primary School, Hampton Hargate

Alyssa Is A Duck

A re we all little ducks
L iving in a big pond with land?
Y ou're a little duck
S o we are all ducks
S upercool
A mazing duck.

Alyssa Barrett (9)
Hampton Hargate Primary School, Hampton Hargate

What It's Like To Be Me!

I am arty and happy
And I like to be merry

I like helping people, I don't mind
Because I like to be kind

I like art
And I have a big heart!

Keerthigaa Senthilkumar (9)
Hampton Hargate Primary School, Hampton Hargate

All About Me

J is for jumping, I like to jump
A is for animals, I love animals
C is for caring, I care for my friends
K is for kindness, I am kind.

Jack TD (9)
Hampton Hargate Primary School, Hampton Hargate

Me

J umping through the trees
A s quick as I can I run
C razy hair everywhere
O n my computer, I game
B ouncing on a trampoline.

Jacob Sloan (9)
Hampton Hargate Primary School, Hampton Hargate

Messy Daisy

D edicated to ballet
A ttempts to do awesome acro
I nternet obsessed
S erious about being a zookeeper
Y oung but very tall.

Daisy Hollingsworth (9)
Hampton Hargate Primary School, Hampton Hargate

Ella

E lla is a super-duper kid
L ollipops she likes
L ong summer walks and leaves falling
A nd kittens are cute with music too.

Ella Raven (9)
Hampton Hargate Primary School, Hampton Hargate

Rugby

R unning free for points
U ltimate matches
G reat, wild and fun
B y far the best ever
Y oung teams are cool!

Harry Flavill (9)

Hampton Hargate Primary School, Hampton Hargate

About When I Was Born

S eptember 7th
O n 2012
F riday was the day
I n Peterborough City Hospital
A t 10.40am, I came along.

Sofia Rodulfo (9)

Hampton Hargate Primary School, Hampton Hargate

Noah

N oah is nice

O bviously loud and funny

A rt is what I'm best at

H elping friends to make them happy.

Noah Ferguson (8)

Hampton Hargate Primary School, Hampton Hargate

This Is Me

Going to the skatepark
Is fun and dangerous
I am happy and cool
I am excited
I loved it
It is good to learn tricks.

Farrell Martinez (9)

Hampton Hargate Primary School, Hampton Hargate

Riley

R eally hard-working

I am very smart

L oving

E nergetic

Y oung.

Riley Flaherty (8)

Hampton Hargate Primary School, Hampton Hargate

This Is Me

S weet as a lump of sugar

H orseriding is my hobby

A nd I don't like saying sorry

N ow! My strengths are talking and horseriding

N oodles are super yummy

O n a Friday night takeaway, yummy in my tummy

N ow for my favourite game. Roblox!

O h, I didn't see you there!

'H orses! Where?

A pples are not as yummy as chocolate cake

G reen grass, blue sky. What a beautiful day!

A mazing! Let's go to the park to play

N ot as fast as everyone else. But my talent is being cute and sassy.

Shannon O'Hagan (10)
Holy Child Primary School, Creggan Estate

This Is Me

K ind. I am very kind
I 'm good at football
L ike, very good
L ike good, good
I also like swimming
A nd video games
N ow I gotta go

D on't leave! I'm here. I was...
O nly joking
H ey! What did you think of my story?
E rm... Are you still there?
R ight... Great
T oday was good
Y es... Seriously? Bye.

Killian Doherty (9)
Holy Child Primary School, Creggan Estate

This Is Me

M y name is Mia
I am such a zebra
A nd I feel like a shooting star

C ool as a cucumber
H appy as can be
A re there people just like me?
M y best friend is Sophia
B ecause we are so close
E veryone knows she likes me the most
R ainbow is my favourite colour
S o maybe I'm not a zebra after all!

Mia Chambers (10)
Holy Child Primary School, Creggan Estate

Happy Bee

Happy Bee, Happy Bee
He is me
Happy Bee is not in his tree
This is me. This is a happy bee for me
I can't see myself in a mirror without feeling guilt
I am good but I hate kilts
I hate winter
Love summer
Not so much the spring
Oh please, oh please
Lend Happy Bee a wing.

Fionn Friel (10)
Holy Child Primary School, Creggan Estate

This Is Me

My name is Bobby
I like boats
They're kind of a hobby
I don't mean to boast
I like... Carpathia
Titanic
I also like dinosaurs
They're kind of fantastic
Atrocoraptor
Pyroraptor
I am Bobbyosaurus.

Bobby (10)
Holy Child Primary School, Creggan Estate

This Is Me

I **A** m Aubree
yo **U** can call me Aubreu
B ecause it's my nickname
R eading and drawing and skipping too
E xtremely lovely and extremely nice
E xtremely, extremely. I said that twice.

Aubree Friel (10)
Holy Child Primary School, Creggan Estate

This Is Me

I am Alfie and I do parkour
I jump like a monkey and hang off the doors
I go to the park and I do some more
I roll like a rock. I roll on the floor
Then I call my friends and do it some more
I am Alfie and I do parkour.

Alfie Gallagher
Holy Child Primary School, Creggan Estate

This Is Me

My name is Jack
I like to game
I play with Tiernan
That's my best friend's name
I mostly play Roblox.
I'm a Problox.

Jack Gallagher (10)
Holy Child Primary School, Creggan Estate

This Is Me

I am Caolan
Excellent at football
Great at running
Nobody knows that I am the best
A good friend
Nobody knows
But I feel great.

Caolan Moore
Holy Child Primary School, Creggan Estate

Bambi: The Roan Pony Mare

Bambi is a roan pony as bright as the sun
She is playful and funny
She was my favourite pony, the only one
Until we moved riding school
I miss Bambi, maybe Bambi misses me
But a pony can't talk, can they?
Now I'm riding different ponies
And I can't believe there's a pony called Darcy
The horse I rode a few weeks ago
Maybe he's my favourite for he trotted for me today
But I'm doing fine, I have been doing lots of drawings
I need to draw Bambi, if only she were mine
We would have a lovely blue set and we'd jump a metre
We'd win competitions
But for now, I'm just a girl who is horse mad!

Darcy Malcomson (10)
St Patrick's Primary School, Hilltown

All 'Bout Me

Here is a poem all 'bout me,
I've got a fluffy cocker spaniel called Ruby.
Here is another thing all 'bout me,
One o' my favourite things is to watch TV.
Here is another thing all 'bout me,
All of my friends call me clumsy.
Got one more minute to listen to me,
I've got two friends called Mads and Sophie.
Oh, one more thing all about me,
Got my hair cut real short, can't you see?
A few more things all 'bout me,
All my friends call me Gracie.
Here is my last thing all 'bout me,
I love, love, love, love, love to read.
Well, folks, that's just all about me.

Grace Gribben (10)
St Patrick's Primary School, Hilltown

This Is Me

I love sport
I play five sports
The sports I play are basketball, Gaelic football,
soccer, hurling and handball.

My family is great
And my dad is the best
But my mum is amazing
I have two sisters
Their names are Niamh and Caoimhe

I like console games
FIFA is the best, Fortnite is alright
I play a Nintendo Switch.

County Down is a great team and proud county
My uncle is the manager
One or more of my relations have won the Sam
Maguire
On each of the 5 occasions, we lifted the cup.

Oisin McConville (10)
St Patrick's Primary School, Hilltown

My Life

F unny as a clown - I am a clown
U nder my bed is really scary
N ever will I like Tyrone
N ever will I like Man United
Y es, I love snooker and pool

O livier Giroud is bad
L ove Man City because they're just good
D o love farming 'cause it gives me something to do

M y family are just great
E ven when I'm naughty.

Patrick Morgan (10)
St Patrick's Primary School, Hilltown

Jake Morgan

J ake Morgan is my name
A nd my favourite team is Man Utd
K itties are not my favourite animal
E very Sunday I go to my nanny's

M y favourite food is pizza
O n my PlayStation I play FIFA
R oast beef I also like
G aming is something I like to do
A nimals I also like
N ew Year's Eve I stay up late.

Jake Morgan (10)
St Patrick's Primary School, Hilltown

How God Made Me

You will need:
A bottle of happiness
A seasoning of life and crazy
A glass of humour
A drop of Italy
And lots of sweets

How to make:
First, get 250ml of happiness
Then get a glass of humour
A seasoning of life and crazy
And a room of sweets
And into the oven
Take out and let cool
Then cut up into pieces
Give a bit for everyone to love.

Oisin McSherry (10)
St Patrick's Primary School, Hilltown

Birthday

B irthdays are my favourite day
I love it when it is my birthday
R espectful is what you should be at my birthday
T he day my birthday is on is in July
H appiness is what I feel on my birthday
D iabetes is what you get at my birthday
A t my birthday I got a bouncy castle
Y ou can go to my birthday.

Austin Matthews (10)

St Patrick's Primary School, Hilltown

This Is Me

Hi, my name is Daniel
Goalkeeping is my favourite thing to do
I like to go to the zoo
Sausages are my favourite food
I love lying in my bed
Milk is my favourite thing to drink
Riding my bike is an exercise to do

Hi, my name is Daniel
I hate Man City
They pay the referee
I want to be a keeper for Liverpool.

Daniel Duggan (9)
St Patrick's Primary School, Hilltown

I Am Tyler

Hello, Tyler is my name
And football is my favourite game
My eyes are blue
And I go to St Patrick's Primary School
I describe myself as happy
But I can be snappy
I like burgers, they are very nice
I also like chicken curry and rice
Going on my tablet is really fun
I like playing with everyone.

Tyler Dinsmore (9)
St Patrick's Primary School, Hilltown

My Birthday

B ouncy castle for one day
I nside it's chaos, people bouncing
R ound and round, having lots of fun
T his cake is amazing!
H ave some more... Yes please!
D own is the theme of the cake
A nd chocolate is the flavour
Y ummy yummy, I love chocolate.

Luke Fearon (10)
St Patrick's Primary School, Hilltown

Me

My name is Ryan
My favourite colour is cyan
My eyes are green
And I like baked beans
Christmas is my favourite holiday
But I also like Easter Sunday
My house is big
And I also like to dig
My dream job is to be a banker
But I also want to be a sailor and let down an anchor.

Ryan Burns (10)
St Patrick's Primary School, Hilltown

I'm Awesome

I like my friend
M y dogs are cute

A re you scared of heights?
W e should be kind
E veryone is different
S mile every day
O n Thursday we're off
M oney isn't everything
E verything nearly is possible.

Jack Binks (9)
St Patrick's Primary School, Hilltown

About Me

Hi, I'm Kelsey and this poem is about me
I like colours and I love dogs
I actually have a dog called Bailey and he is so cute
I also like football, camogie and the team Liverpool
My favourite food is pizza and I like fizzy drinks
And that's the end of my story all about me.

Kelsey Quinn (10)
St Patrick's Primary School, Hilltown

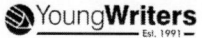

Sport

S occer, hurling, football, basketball, I love them all

P laying sport with my friends is just the best feeling in the world

O bviously Man United are the best soccer team

R oom for improvement in hurling and football

T rying my best always.

Senan Quinn (10)

St Patrick's Primary School, Hilltown

This Is Me

T o play football
H appy, kind, healthy
I t is my pleasure to farm
S it in front of the fire

I t is my pleasure to have to
S ee my family

M eet up with my cousins
E lephants are smelly.

Ryan Devlin (10)
St Patrick's Primary School, Hilltown

Alan's Amazing Day!

Hi, I'm Alan, this is me.
Every morning I drink tea!
I go to school and I have fun.
When it's break time I play with the ball.
Then when I try to catch it I run, run, run!
When I go home I eat, I eat lunch.
Potatoes, chicken, it's a bunch!
When I play my games I'm a winner.
Would you look at that! It's time for dinner.
I go to the campfire and sleep in a den.
Then the day cycle starts all over again!

Alan Cychowski (10)
Sunny Bank Primary School, Sittingbourne

About Me And My Hopes Of The Future

I hope I work with animals in a zoo too!
Training, feeding, petting, lots of cuddles too!
My zoo would be where you pet and feed
Do you want your child to be filled with glee?
You have to pay more for them to come out and take a picture with you
Say cheese!
In the zoo, dolphins too!
The animals are crystals shining in the sunlight
You will see animals of all kinds too!
The sun will be as gold as our smiles too.

Chloe Eustace (10)

Sunny Bank Primary School, Sittingbourne

My Feelings

I show my good emotions
Not my true feelings
When you see my face
I have a smile
But on the inside
My smile is miles

I have friends
But not many
I have a few
But not a lot
But they are mine
And I wouldn't give them up for the world.

Lizziemarie Wilson (10)
Sunny Bank Primary School, Sittingbourne

All About Me

L ots of smiles

I nvincible

L ots of kindness

L ots of shyness

Y ou always be you

D oesn't give up

O pen-minded

Y ou always make me smile

L ots of helpfulness

E very day smiles.

Lilly Doyle (9)

Sunny Bank Primary School, Sittingbourne

A Recipe Of Amelia

What makes me:
500g of glee
190g of positivity
12kg of smiles that glow
250kg of the face everybody knows
A jugful of shining sapphire eyes
505g of sunset-yellow hair

Use this recipe
To make one me.

Amelia Bolger (9)
Sunny Bank Primary School, Sittingbourne

This Imaginary World

Sometimes I imagine what I could be
In this imaginary world, I can see...
I feel like I can fly in the wonderful sky
And leave the true world and say goodbye
I dive in the water as I do
And animals swim with me too.

Oliver Glenn (10)
Sunny Bank Primary School, Sittingbourne

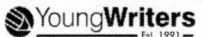

Words To Describe Darcy

D inky, daring, darling and delighted
A ccepting, achieving, ambitious and aggressive
R eady, relaxed, reliable and remarkable
C alm, caring, cautious and champion
Y oung and yearning.

Darcy Price (9)

Sunny Bank Primary School, Sittingbourne

Hi, I'm George!

I'm George
I like games and stuff that doesn't make me bored
I love to have fun and play with my friends
When school ends I go in my mum's car
And I go home and sometimes the park.

George Butler (10)
Sunny Bank Primary School, Sittingbourne

Me, Payton

I'm ambitious. I'm smart
I like air hockey and art
I have brown eyes and brown hair
I have freckles and my skin is fair
I like drawing and anime
I also really love Saturday!

Payton Grimwood (10)
Sunny Bank Primary School, Sittingbourne

All About Me

D eclan is my name
E njoy YouTube daily
C aring about my family
L aughing at memes
A nd I live in my bedroom
N ow you know all about me.

Declan Bruce (9)

Sunny Bank Primary School, Sittingbourne

I Am Me

My name is Taylor
My eyes are blue
I am special just like you
I may be loud
But there is one thing that makes me proud
I have autism.

Taylor Friday (10)
Sunny Bank Primary School, Sittingbourne

My Name Is Riley

My name is Riley
I am a bit ambitious
I am amazing at playing football
I am rubbish at fighting
I am great at writing.

Riley (10)
Sunny Bank Primary School, Sittingbourne

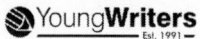

Jemma

J ealous all the time
E mbraces feelings
M ischievous
M emorable
A rtistic.

Jemma Tyler-Clarke (10)
Sunny Bank Primary School, Sittingbourne

YoungWriters®
Est. 1991

YOUNG WRITERS
INFORMATION

We hope you have enjoyed reading this book – and that you will continue to in the coming years.

If you're the parent or family member of an enthusiastic poet or story writer, do visit our website **www.youngwriters.co.uk/subscribe** and sign up to receive news, competitions, writing challenges and tips, activities and much, much more! There's lots to keep budding writers motivated!

If you would like to order further copies of this book, or any of our other titles, then please give us a call or order via your online account.

Young Writers
Remus House
Coltsfoot Drive
Peterborough
PE2 9BF
(01733) 890066
info@youngwriters.co.uk

Join in the conversation!
Tips, news, giveaways and much more!

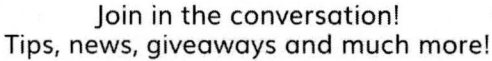

 YoungWritersUK    YoungWritersCW    youngwriterscw